The Road to Serenity

The Road to Serenity

EMILY AKLAN

StoryTerrace

Text Julie Abrams-Humphries, on behalf of StoryTerrace

Design StoryTerrace

Copyright © Emily Aklan

Text is private and confidential

First print May 2022

StoryTerrace

www.StoryTerrace.com

The power of kindness is so far-reaching and long-lasting—if you can save a life, you can save a generation.

– Emily Aklan,
printed in the Autumn 2021
edition of Global Woman's Magazine

Contents

Preface

The path out of tragedy is hard. Loss is difficult and devastating, but it can lead to hope. When my lovely sister, Faye, passed away suddenly in her thirties, I was faced with the dilemma of reclaiming her daughters. Through this experience and those I had encountered in the early days of Serenity Welfare, I was led further into the social care system in England, and I was horrified by what I found. It made me more determined to make a difference, to improve the whole experience for children caught up in the system.

If Faye had not passed away, there would be no Serenity Welfare, and I want to show people that out of great loss and pain, something incredible has evolved to help vulnerable children and young people.

This book chronicles my personal journey and showcases the work that Serenity Welfare does. It tells of the epiphany that led to a change of direction in my career, which led to the campaign Hope Instead of Handcuffs. I believe I chose the right path. As a daughter of immigrants making their own way in the world, when I recently stepped off the plane from North Cyprus, it was a humbling experience to receive the Gold Award as Best Business Woman of the Year in the children and families category, and many thanks must go to all who helped me on my journey.

To my beautiful angel in heaven, Faye. You were taken from us too soon, but I know God had a plan for the greater good. I know you help children and young people up there as I do down here, and I thank you for allowing me to bring up your beautiful girls. I want to thank my family and friends. Without them, I would not have been the strong woman I am today. All my challenges were given as lessons; without them, none of our successes would have been possible.

I must thank my staff and external partners. Without our great team, Serenity Welfare could not serve the children and young people it does so well. Your passion and dedication are truly outstanding, and I know we have left a positive imprint on hundreds of lives over the years. I am truly proud to be steering this ship with you all on board! May we continue to serve humanity for generations to come.

1
Little Bags

'Every one of us needs to show how much we care for each other and, in the process, care for ourselves.'

Diana, Princess of Wales

A new chapter of my life began with a conversation. It was a chill, dark February day in 2017, and we had been called to securely transport a vulnerable child from a hospital mental assessment unit in the north and back down to Hertfordshire. We arrived in a sleek black Mercedes GLA. It was a heated cocoon of luxury, part of a fleet we'd used since Serenity Welfare started in November of the previous year. The sort of vehicle you'd more likely see whisking celebrities through city streets than transporting a young person in social care, but I was determined that those young people should be treated well. Were they not just as deserving of dignity and respect as others? Why should they be transported in battered transit vans when there was a better alternative? It wasn't the first such journey we had made, but it was the first where I had encountered the appalling treatment of children in care.

In contrast to our vehicle, the assessment centre was a functional building, a bleak hospital unit, and once we gained access, it was difficult to find our young person. Every ward looked the same, cold and white, and every room of those wards drab and clinical. Eventually, we came across him, and I was shocked by what we found. Backed into the opposite corner of a small room, behind a couple of nurses, was a child, no more than 12 years old, shabbily dressed and dirty. It was obvious he hadn't washed for days. By his feet were all his worldly possessions, shoved into two black bin bags. Underneath a mop of unruly hair, he had the most angelic face and fair skin, deep-set with beautiful blue eyes. Eyes that glared at us, full of hostility. He was extremely distressed with a frightened look in his eyes and adamantly refused to be transported; he said so in no uncertain terms. We have a different ethos from other providers, and I countered his defiance with a softer tone.

'It's OK, we can't force you to come with us. We'll wait outside for 15 minutes. If you come, you come. If you don't, we'll try another day.'

We retreated outside. A few minutes went by, and I became aware that someone was standing in the doorway, watching us, two little bags at his feet.

'I'm ready to go,' he said, sheepishly. The poor boy was carrying more emotional baggage than would have filled his bin bags. In care from the age of three, with autism and ADHD, the risk assessment had said. I'm glad he chose to communicate with me that day. 'Can I have a cigarette?' he asked as he spotted a dob end on the floor and bent to pick it up.

'I can't give you one, and don't pick that up from the floor,' I replied. He lit it anyway.

'But it calms me down.' I opened the door to the Mercedes.

'Well, you can't smoke in the car.'

'This car?' He dropped the cigarette. 'Oh my god, are we going in this?' he said. I smiled back at him in assurance. 'Wow! I've never been in a car like this. I feel special.' He slid gratefully in the back next to the transport officer as I put his bags in the boot. He ran a hand along the leather interior as I started the engine. 'This is so wicked,' he said.

We'd been driving for a while, streets and buildings slipping past as the roads opened out towards the home counties, before he asked my name.

'Emily,' I answered. 'And I know what your name is. This is my colleague, Steve.' The boy nodded and seemed to think for a moment.

'Emily, I'm sorry I was rude to you in the hospital. I thought you were going to force me to come.' I glanced in the rear-view mirror as he raised his hands, red welts circling his wrists. 'Like the company who took me to that place, they put me in handcuffs,' he said. I tried to focus on the road, my eyes clouded with tears. I'd heard of children being handcuffed in secure transportation, but I'd never seen the evidence. I took a deep breath and steadied my voice.

'I'm sorry you had to go through that. You know we would never handcuff you. That's not the way we work.' He smiled a little then.

'That's OK, Emily. I realised you were different when you told me you were just going to wait outside.'

It was an emotional four-hour journey, and when we passed the county sign for Hertfordshire, he recognised it.

'My mum lived here,' he said, and his energy dipped at the memory. He hung his head until we reached our destination. I dropped him off, and he said he would see me again. Later, as I was unloading the car, I found his jacket in the boot, so I drove back. I was met by the grinning 12-year-old.

'Hello, Mercedes woman. Told you I'd see you again, didn't I?'

That young person's situation gave me a lot to think about. It wasn't like I didn't know handcuffs were used, often by private, secure transportation companies, for children who were not criminals or offenders, strapping their feet in plastic bonds or wrists in soft or metal handcuffs, but I had never seen the evidence first-hand. It made me sick. An idea rooted in my mind that one day, I would do something about this barbaric practice. I would start a campaign to stop this inhumane treatment, and that is how Hope Instead of Handcuffs was born.

Children in care will be driven to appointments in luxury Mercedes

GOODIE BAGS CONTAINING SNACKS AND A MAGAZINE ARE ALSO PROVIDED, FINDS NICOLA TAYLOR

Serenity Welfare: first article highlighting the first ever service transporting children in care in high-end vehicles

Call to stop caging our kids in care

EXCLUSIVE

By **Lucy Johnston** HEALTH EDITOR

CHILDREN in care as young as 11 are being handcuffed and treated like "dangerous animals", warn politicians who are demanding the practice be banned.

A cross-party coalition of MPs and peers is calling for an end to cages, restraints and handcuffs during the transport of non-custodial children in care.

The 26 MPs have backed a campaign – Hope instead of Handcuffs – demanding the Government bans the practice, which is routinely used by some operators, "unless there is a considerable risk of the child harming themselves or others". The call, backed by a report released today, says the Government must introduce an approach "that treats vulnerable children as victims instead of criminals".

It follows a review of social care which said the social services system often weakens rather than strengthens a child's support networks.

The Independent Review of Children's Social Care found the majority of families seeking support were struggling in conditions of adversity, rather than abusing or neglecting their children. Josh MacAlister, who led the review, described the system as a "tower of Jenga held together with Sellotape".

Labour MP Steve McCabe, chair of the All-Party Parliamentary Group on looked-after children and care leavers, will table an early day motion demanding an end to the practice. He said: "Children as young as 11 are being put in handcuffs for even short journeys.

"This is no way to treat children in care who are supposed to be getting protection. It sounds like the way you would treat dangerous animals."

Emily Aklan, of Serenity Welfare which runs a national transport service for looked-after children, said: "If you strolled up outside the school and put your child in handcuffs you would have social services or the police over in minutes."

'It is no way to treat children'

Sunday Express article for the Hope instead of Handcuffs campaign

2
Pieces Of Each Other –
Our Childhood

'We are nothing without each other, and it's time that we admit we are actually pieces of each other.'

Lidia Yuknavitch

I n the drawing room of our Serenity Welfare head office, between two bay windows that look out over the front lawns, hangs an oil painting in a heavy gilt frame. It shows children in traditional dress skipping and dancing beside a donkey, led by a woman, as they return from the harvest. Painted in the classical style by William Adolphe Bouguereau in 1878, it is a celebratory, loving piece of work and could easily be of a family group. It was hanging in situ when we viewed the property and decided to make it our base. The painting is a reflection of family, which is at the heart of everything we do. My background and family tell the story of how I got to this place.

I was born in Holloway, North London in 1971 at the maternity hospital near to our house on Marlborough Road. My parents gave me the birth name Emine, but I came to be known as Emily. My parents, Sapriye and Yakup, came to Britain in the 1960s along with many other Turkish Cypriots after war broke out in 1964. They met and married in the UK in 1967. It was an arranged marriage, and I recall hearing my mum say she didn't fancy my father when she first saw him.

'But I learned to love him!' she said. My mother was something of a looker in her day. With her smouldering looks and dark hair piled high walking down Holloway Road, she was often mistaken for Sophia Loren. Although Mum's given name was Sapriye, she was renamed after her aunty, so people knew her as Fikriye. She was younger than my father, Yakup, who was in his early 20s when they married. I came along two years later and was named after my grandmother on my paternal side. Four years later, my sister arrived, named after my maternal grandmother – Fayize. We called her Faye for short.

There may have been four years, but there was barely any distance between us sisters. We were close, we looked alike, and Mum dressed us like peas in a pod in the same outfits with the same hair. That was all right when I was little, but I hated it when I got older, and at 13 I still had my hair in plaits like my little sister. When I reached my teens, I put my foot down about the matching outfits and nagged until Mum finally agreed to let us go shopping up at Tammy Girl, Chelsea Girl and Dorothy Perkins, where we'd get high-waisted jeans and bangles like Madonna.

By the time I was born, there were over 100,000 Turkish Cypriots in Britain and a strong Turkish community where we were growing up near Palmers Green. We were close as immediate and extended family, with grandparents, aunts and uncles. Sundays were a big family event, often at our house, which was the hub for everyone. Mum cooked lavish roast dinners, and in the summer months, we would have a barbeque that started at 9 a.m. and carried on well into the night. I was expected to do a lot of the domestic chores and help at these events, so I was always rushed off my feet and waiting on the family hand and foot. There was a little less to do on our picnic days out, when a convoy of family cars would make their way through the Essex roads out to Tilbury or Southend, and we'd stop and picnic in fields along the way.

Dad worked all week as a Hoffman presser in the rag trade, and Mum was a machinist at home. When Faye and I were teenagers, our parents started their own business: a dry cleaner in Dagenham. Dad did the pressing, and Mum did the alterations. We were with them at work or left to our own devices, and when we were little, my dad's mum looked after us. By the time I was 14, a neighbour looked in. She became like an aunty to us and taught me how to cook.

Faye and I clashed when we were young, repelling like two magnetic North Poles; we fought like cat and dog, especially over the house chores. Growing up, I was the introvert, a follower of rules, whereas Faye would rebel against them. I would do as I was told and get on with it, and Faye didn't. I'd climb upstairs and clean, thinking she was doing the same downstairs, but when I got there, she had done nothing.

'You don't do anything! I've done all the upstairs,' I'd yell and we'd argue, and all hell would break loose! Although Faye and I fought, I was still defensive of her; she was my little sister after all. Open-hearted and kind, her choice of friends was sometimes suspect. Faye was easily led and attracted people who exploited her kindness. I looked out for her.

At the end of a school day, I was the one who did my homework and made sure the table was laid like every day was Groundhog Day. I grew up quickly because of my responsibilities. It was a part of the Turkish culture; our community believed a woman's place was in the home, complying with domestic duties, while the men went out working or gambling. People were set in their ways. I saw my mum work 12-to-13-hour days while the men had more freedom.

That impacted me in later life. I made a career for myself and wanted to be independent of a man, but the family influence remained strong. At Serenity Welfare, I wanted to create a warm family environment for vulnerable children at our base. I wanted it to be a place full of people who spoke pleasantly and respectfully to each other, regardless of background. Even if the children had come from a background of anger and explosions of physical violence, we wanted them to feel safe, cossetted even. They deserved that. As if they were part of a proper, warm, loving family, as happy as the portrait in the drawing room.

Family life was happy growing up, and I sailed through my schooling. Faye and I went to the same primary school, then were separated, as I went to an all-girls school in Enfield, and she went to a mixed secondary in the same area. But Faye was bullied there, so Mum stepped in and transferred her close to our dry cleaners in Dagenham. Sadly, she was bullied again. Faye had a darker skin colour than mine, and maybe that was picked up on, as she was the victim of racist insults from some of the other children. One day, Mum was called to the school because Faye had snapped and put one of the abuser's heads down the toilet. The school did not expel her, but they put her on suspension pending investigation, so they did take it seriously. We had seen shuttered shops with racist graffiti in Dagenham, but we were not affected as a family. They seemed to leave our shop alone.

I didn't have to experience the issues my sister did, but we were at different schools. I kept my head down and studied, while Faye was chatty in class and would speak out and get into trouble. I made close friends at school and remained in contact with them for some time, and I made more when I went to Barnet College in 1986 to take business studies. Then I finished college and started to work in the offices of Harrods as a mail-order clerk, while Faye lived at home and went to college in Enfield, where she met J.

When Faye was born, in 1975

Emily, Faye and grandad and grandmother

Emily as a baby with auntie

Mum and dad at their wedding registry, 1967

3

Pieces Of Someone Else

'You must be the change you wish to see in the world.'

Gandhi

had two years at Barnet College. It was my first time in mixed-gender education, and although it was a bit of a cultural shock for me, I liked it, and I made new male and female friends. When I left, I had the idea that I would get a job at Harrods, a British icon, and use my newly acquired business studies degree to work my way up. The store was in a new phase, having been bought in 1985 by the businessman Al Fayed, an outsider to the British 'establishment', who dropped the royal warrant from Harrods when he said not doing so would be hypocritical, as neither the Queen nor Prince Charles had shopped there for several years.

I was interviewed, and they turned me down twice. I

suppose I was only 17 or 18, and they weren't prepared to take me seriously, but I wanted the job so badly, I would be damned if I didn't get in.

'Please give me a chance. I can do this job. Give me three months.' I pleaded. They did and started me in international mail orders. Pre-internet, it was a complex job, filling a multitude of forms in triplicate, taking orders over the phone, dealing with internal memos, and filling many brown envelopes that were whisked away by post trolleys and delivered to all the different Harrods departments. The year after I joined, Al Fayed introduced a dress code for customers that banned anyone wearing cycling shorts or flip-flops. I left for work early, suited and booted in my smartest attire, taking the 23 stops on the Piccadilly Line there, and home at the end of the day. It was a dusty old rattling line, even then.

When I passed my driving test, I decided to treat myself to my first car, and bought a sporty XR3i Ford convertible. I drove to park at Arnos Grove station and took the train in from there, which cut my commuting time down a little. I worked long hours at Harrods, scurrying between the underground tunnels that linked all the offices, departments and warehouses below Brompton Road, my string of pearls clinking and big hair threatening to collapse unless I kept it up with regular bursts of hairspray in the ladies' room. I wore the power, dressing so synonymously with the '80s, the boxy 'Chanel' style tweed jackets and chains. I may have looked the part, but I was still naïve and young. It was over the years that AIDS was prevalent. I didn't know there was a big gay scene in London, and I had lots of friends who were handsome men. I had no idea they were gay.

There were bonuses to working for the world's best department store. If I got in before nine and headed to the food hall, I could buy the chocolates they couldn't sell the night before for next to nothing. I also had a Harrods staff card, which you were expected to use in-store, and I bought tights from the hosiery department and other items. Al Fayed was clever; he sold the card to staff as a bonus, but we were basically putting our wages straight back into his store.

I stayed at Harrods for 18 months, until I was introduced to a second cousin who had come over from North Cyprus. My parents thought he might make a good match as a husband. I had worked for my independence, and it was about to be taken away from me. I wasn't happy about it at all, and he didn't even have a UK passport, but my parents worked on me. They persuaded me it would be a good move. We were married in London within six months of our first meeting.

Our wedding was in March. Large and traditional, it was mostly organised by my mother; I didn't have much say. I tried to get my wedding dress made in the style of Princess Diana's, with a long train and puffy sleeves, but I was re-directed to the only style of dress that our local Turkish dressmaker in Holloway did: heavily embroidered and heavy to wear. I did get my train, although it was twelve feet, not 20 feet long. The wedding was at a registry office, and the reception was held in a London hotel with 500 guests and a 12-tier cake. I didn't know half the people there. When the dancing started, the guests threw money. At the end of the evening, a huge line snaked through the room as everyone lined up to pin notes to my dress, as was tradition. I could barely move; my feet were aching, my smile fixed, and I was so hot. Although it was an extravagant and beautiful wedding, I can't say I enjoyed it much.

In June of the same year, we did it all over again, with my husband's family in North Cyprus. The same dress and a similar ceremony, but in 42 degrees of heat. If I had felt hot in the dress in London in March, now I had my own personal dress sauna. I stood all day, had one glass of lemonade and was ready to go home, but I had the line of well-wishers with their money ready to endure first. By the time we were finished, I had effectively been through about three weddings. My husband and I only got to know each other after it all finished. He didn't speak English, and I didn't speak Turkish, but we managed. He's a lovely guy, and we are still married.

After the first wedding, he moved in with me and my parents. After the Turkish ceremony in North Cyprus, we moved into the flat above the dry cleaners in Dagenham. It was a nice, big flat, but we were still so young, and as a married woman, I was not expected to work, so I had to leave Harrods. Then I fell pregnant, which was a total shock to the system. I had no prior experience with men, and I went to my mum to complain.

'I'm too young for this. We've only just got married.' She made it clear that I had no choice.

'You have to have this child. We do not allow abortions in this family.' I was still just out of childhood myself. It was a difficult pregnancy through a hot summer during which I suffered from water retention and high blood pressure. My feet were the size of balloons and uncomfortable, and I ended up in hospital for the third trimester. It was a relief when I went into labour, but I had a horrendous birth experience. Thankfully, by the end of it all, I had a beautiful 6lb 9oz baby girl. There were difficulties with family over the naming of our daughter. Mum wanted her to have her name; my husband wanted a new name. He registered her as S, and the next day I went to the registry office and changed it; he went back and changed it again. We had a massive row and nearly split up because of the naming of our child. She's now 30, and still one half of the family call her S, and the other call her F.

Meanwhile, my sister had left school and started college. While I shifted into the role of a wife and mother, she became the rebellious one. She met a Greek boy at Enfield College, J, and fell in love. As far as our family were concerned, that was a total no-no; there was no love lost between Greek and Turkish Cypriots, and a history of conflict on both sides. Faye and J absconded several times to his parents' house. He had an English mother and a Greek Cypriot father. Mum and other family members went out looking for her; when they found out she was seeing a Greek boy, they went mad. They got her home and tried to lock her in her room and stop her from going to college. They gave a warning to J to leave Faye alone. The couple were pulled apart by family, both heartbroken.

That situation pushed my sister off the rails. Afterwards, she would go out for days, running with the wrong crowd, coming home late and rebelling. That went on for a few years and put the whole family in uproar, and she dropped all her education. Later, she met a Turkish Cypriot; they ended up marrying, much to the family's relief (although it did not turn out well), and she had her two children, who are my nieces.

I had a young child of my own by this time. She was about nine when Faye had her first child, N, in 2000. Our roles swapped again after Faye's next daughter, I, was born two years later. I became a career woman and Faye the stay-at-home mum. A friend who worked for a well-known chain of estate agents in the early '90s asked me if I wanted a job. I thought it sounded good, I could give it a try. There was resistance from my family, who thought I should stay at home and be a mother, like my sister, but I remained resolute, and went to work at the estate agents with long fair hair that matched my sister's golden locks, Chanel style jackets and the powerful dressing that I'd started at Harrods.

I became more ambitious and career orientated, and I wanted to earn more. My husband was OK with it, but my mum was resistant; she didn't think construction was a suitable role for women. It was a male-dominated industry, and she would often make comments about it. Mum was my childcare, so I tried to appease her. By the time my daughter was in late primary, I had to get a live-in au pair, Anna, who was with us for three years. This didn't go down well with the rest of the family, who thought I should be the main caregiver. My husband was a tailor by trade, and he had his own shop by then, so he was busy.

After about 18 months, I transitioned into the new homes department in Queensbury and Kingsbury, near Stanmore and the Wembley area, which meant joining the construction industry. I had a lot to juggle: a daughter at school, a long commute, and long hours. Those eased when I transferred to Enfield, and our family moved there. In the new homes department, I began working on a development at Cockfosters. It was around the time of the property boom, and I was associated with the prestigious builder Charles Church.

I was determined to make a career for myself in construction. There were so few women in the business, so you had to really prove yourself, and I was driven enough to be noticed. Women were still at the heart of the home then, and I thought we had a better eye for designing new homes to be functional and practical, putting in his and hers basins in en suites and a dining area in the kitchen. I really wanted to get my teeth into these issues at the production stage. I wanted the right properties built in the right locations, so I made sure I was in the planning stage of development.

Women in the housing industry were found in new homes sales offices, but not in planning or on site. This was changing. I realised I didn't want to be a commodity and get whistled at by workers hanging off scaffolding. I wanted to be useful and show what skills I had. I made the site offices take down all the Page Three girls' calendars and put policies in place to protect women and their rights.

At the age of 32 I became a sales project manager, a young age in construction to take up such a position. I was given a blue Vauxhall Astra as a company car, which was more commonly associated with Essex wide boys! I spent a lot of time travelling from site to site across a big territory covering the whole of South East England. The more successful the build projects were, the more work I was given. I moved house builders when I was 36 and was put on the board at a house building company when I attended my first board meeting. It was full of middle-aged white men. I don't think they knew what to make of me and my dynamic approach.

By the early 2000s, technology was taking off, and the country was heading into a recession. It was harder to buy land, build and sell, so we had to adapt our approach. I found my new ideas were not well received. I marketed some terrible brownfield sites, rebranding the new homes as 'sex in the city'. They were modern, upside-down townhouses designed by men who had no consideration for how many times you had to be running up and down the stairs from the kitchen to the first and second floor. Nobody spent money on those developments with a view of a housing estate and the burned-out cars in Hackney. It was pre-gentrification; Islington was at its peak, the Blairs lived there, and we were getting an overflow of young professionals into the area, as was Hackney. My campaign was fresh and sexy. I hired the platforms at London Liverpool Street train station and bombarded the tsunami of commuters with shiny leaflets, breaking ground in a very established industry. Although the board couldn't get their heads around the marketing campaign, it worked. We pulled in young, affluent buyers and sold six of the houses in two months with the property prices reaching in excess of £700,000.

In 2005 I reached my year-end targets and got an amazing bonus in the middle of a recession. It was to be my last year working as an employee. I started to branch out on my own. It took a lot of courage to leave a six-figure salary and start again, and my parents thought I was bonkers, but I had decided to consult, to give my knowledge back to the public and open my own company. I would be a property doctor, and Aklan International was born, a place that combined property psychology with sales. I consulted for housebuilders abroad, making sure regulations were in place, and I acted on behalf of individual members of the public as an advocate. It was the time when female-led property programmes starring Sarah Beeny and Kirsty Allsop were on the rise, and I started to gather interest in the media. There was a four-page article in *The Telegraph*, and the phones did not stop ringing after that. I had my own property column and national newspaper coverage and was called 'a professional, no-nonsense talker; she certainly knows how estate agents' minds work'.

I said, 'Agents respond readily if they find you speak their language.' I became the translator for the layman client and advocated a little healthy competition. Why put your property on the market with one company when you could have it with a few?

In the late 2000s I went international when I was asked to go to Bamako in Mali, West Africa for a government project. There I saw incredible poverty and experienced a life so different from mine in England. International companies had flooded in because of the country's gold and diamond reserves, but the people had nothing. We were dealing with an old French colony and the remnants of that corruption within the government and were trying to do some good to improve the shocking state of public housing.

I stayed in The Radisson with a lot of other foreigners, where there was always a sense of danger, the threat of kidnap just beyond the doors of the hotel. Our project was rewarding; we were knocking down mud houses and rebuilding social housing with better sanitation, but I was away from home for long periods of time over three years while my daughter was in her mid-teens and my husband was working. I'd come back to the UK and buy shoes and chocolate to take to the children in Mali. It was a humbling experience and one of the biggest challenges I had undertaken, but also one of the most rewarding. It showed me what I was capable of, the strength that would be invaluable in the years to come.

Towards the end of the project, I got ill with some sub-Saharan disease and was sent home. There were only three flights a week, and I'd missed them, so I had to fly back via Libya, which was in the middle of a war. When we stopped to change planes, I felt intimidated in a chaotic airport full of men with machine guns, packed with foreigners trying to get out. I joined the end of a long queue at passport control, and an army officer came over. He took my passport and read my name, surprised that I was British.

'But your name is Emine,' he said.

'Yes.'

'Where are you from?'

'I'm from London, but Turkish,' I answered nervously.

'Ah, you from Turkey – I love the Turkish football team Galatasaray. Come, come with me.' I followed, wondering where he was taking me. Was I to be one of the Westerners that were kidnapped? I had no choice but to go with him as he escorted me to the front of the long queue and pushed me in front of an aggressive-looking passport officer. The soldier handed over my passport. The officer glanced at it, glowering, a cigarette smouldering from the corner of his mouth. Then his face lit up.

'You carry the prophet's mother's name – Aminah,' he said. Emine is spelled the same in Turkish and Arabic but has a different pronunciation. I was led to the plane feeling I had had a lucky escape. By the time we touched down at Heathrow, I wanted to kiss the floor!

Emily working in Mali, Africa

Emily and Faye, June 2009

Emily aged 34; the property days

Family memories

4
Losing Faye

'No one ever told me that grief felt so like fear.'
'You care so much; you feel as though you will bleed to death with the pain of it.'
'Only people who are capable of loving strongly can also suffer great sorrow, but this same necessity of loving serves to counteract their grief and heals them.'

Unknown

My sister's life ran alongside mine. While I carved out a career, she had her two girls; N was born in 2000 with the most beautiful eyes, as blue as the Mediterranean, the only one in our family with blue eyes. She was born a few months after our grandmother, my mum's mum, passed away. After her daughter's birth, Faye saw our grandmother in a dream and told her, 'Well done on the baby girl and those beautiful blue eyes.'

Faye seemed happy being at home while her husband worked with our parents in the dry cleaners. Her husband was the right sort of husband for them, a Turkish Cypriot and, they thought, a steadying influence after Faye's younger rebelliousness. He and Faye lived with our parents for a while, then bought a house in Rainham, Essex, with the proceeds from the money pinned to Faye's wedding dress. After a good couple of years, Faye became pregnant with her second daughter, I. It was a difficult birth; I was tangled in the cord, and she couldn't breathe at first. She had bad reflux as a baby, and it was hard to find anything she could keep down. Faye had her in a constant supply of bibs and fresh clothes, but she was such a happy child. Faye copied our mother and dressed her girls in the same way. I asked her why, as we never liked it when she did it to us! N and I were as different in character as we had been. N was expressive and forthright, and I happy-go-lucky and laid-back. They have stayed the same in adulthood.

As years went by, Faye took on the duties that fell to me when I was younger. She was always cooking and made a big effort with family occasions; Christmas was a huge thing for her. She never minded being the centre of attention for those events, while I never liked it. Then my parents decided they would return to North Cyprus to retire. They sold the shop in Dagenham and gave the other shop in Rainham to

Faye's husband to run. It was a profitable business and a generous gift.

When I was away in Africa, Faye's daughters started school just round the corner from their house, and Faye was left home alone, as slowly, slowly, her husband went out for longer and longer periods. He would take his phone with him, one of those heavy brick style mobiles, but was unavailable when Faye tried to call it. He never called home to say where he was or when he'd be back, and he began to disengage with his family. When the family picked up on this, Faye covered for him. She said he'd popped out or was upstairs in the bath and couldn't come down; these were the tales she told us when he hadn't been home for days.

Eventually, Faye discovered he had been conducting an affair with one of her friends, and she called me, screaming her head off. That friend had been at their wedding. How could she do such a thing? Of course, he denied everything, but the other woman became obsessed with him, and she called Faye up, detailing dates and times when they had met and telling her how they had sex and where, really digging the knife in. Faye's husband left. He spent most of his time with the other woman and hardly saw his children, leaving my sister with no income or child support. She had nothing to cover the bills or buy food with.

Shortly after I returned from Africa, Faye fell into a deep depression. One day, I received a call from her neighbour.

'You need to come over right away; the ambulance is

here. Your sister tried to take her life.' I jumped in the car and drove from Barnet to Rainham like a woman possessed. She was just getting into the ambulance, and she told the paramedics and me, 'It's all right, I just had a panic attack.' She was covering up, as the children were still in the house. I realised then how serious the situation had become.

After that, Faye confided in me. She told me the woman had told her, 'If you are that good a wife, why is your husband spending all his time with me?' Her cruel remarks shattered Faye. I was angry with her for trying to handle the whole thing by herself; she had no immediate family nearby, and our parents were abroad, but I was her sister – she should have told me. I found brown envelopes from the bailiffs in the hall that had been flung to one side, and I opened them and realised just how bad things were. I confronted her husband.

'How dare you just leave and leave my sister with nothing? It's not even your shop. My dad left it to you so you could look after your family.' He wasn't interested. He had been too busy setting up a new life.

I had to let my parents know what was going on then, and as soon as I told them, our dad flew back. And he went to the shop and tried to reason with Faye's husband. My parents found it scandalous that this was happening; it was a betrayal of their good faith in him, and against all their principles. The other woman was not willing to let our family get 'her man' back; he was a lucrative source of income, and we discovered later he was about the fifth person in the trail of men she had targeted. She was a gold digger and a con artist, but Faye's husband refused to believe a bad word against her.

Dad stayed on for a while to support Faye, but her health deteriorated. Her husband came back to her, so Dad, thinking it was sorted, returned to North Cyprus. It wasn't long before the husband started leaving Faye again and the phone calls started up. The other woman rang Faye and described intimate acts in full detail. Then Faye's husband packed his bag and left for good.

When I visited Faye on impulse one day, I found her lying on the sofa. She had not washed for days, and the children had not eaten; it looked like they hadn't washed for days either. The whole house was a tip.

'Oh my god, Faye,' I said. 'This has to stop. You and the children go to Mum and Dad. I'll sort this mess out, sell the house and deal with the bastard. You are not staying here any longer.' I organised the flights and got them on a plane to North Cyprus, where they stayed for the next five years.

I had a battle on my hands to negotiate with the husband to sell their house. He believed he was entitled to everything (although he'd arrived into the UK from North Cyprus with nothing), and everything had been given to him by my family. I told him the house would be sold and I would give my sister the proceeds; he had left her with nothing else. After a prolonged battle in which he didn't ask about the children, as he did not want to know, he finally agreed. I sold the house for a decent profit and sent the proceeds of the sale to North Cyprus. Faye bought a house there, and her children started school. Faye continued to struggle with depression for years and still yearned for her husband. She could not accept what happened or move on.

Finally, five years passed, and Faye met an English guy in North Cyprus and fell in love. My parents were not too happy, as she had been through so much. Perhaps they worried it would happen again. But she achieved a divorce from her former husband, and she and M got engaged. He moved in with her and the children. Things were looking up for her; she was happy for the first time in a long time and had started work. M could not get a work visa out there, so they decided to return to the UK.

In November 2010, the two of them came back and stayed with me for a few months while they sorted a place to live and work and schools for the girls. M was a chef, so he found a job quickly, and the girls came over for Christmas, so we were all together. In February, we found a new build house close to where I lived in Enfield for their family. As Faye and I sat sorting through the paperwork and planning the payment of the council tax, she turned to me and said, 'When it's my funeral, Emily, I want two white doves released, and a black marble headstone with two white doves resting on top.' This was completely out of the blue.

'What are you talking about, Faye? Why are we talking about this now?'

'I'm just telling you.' She paused. 'I want white lilies and other white flowers, and I want all my friends to come to my funeral too,' she said. I was a bit taken aback.

'Is there something you need to tell me, Faye? Are you going somewhere?'

'No, I'm just telling you,' she said.

'Well, I'm shutting this conversation down right now. I won't have this discussion with you; it's irrelevant.' That is the last we spoke of it.

Faye moved into her new home at the beginning of March 2011, and it was an exciting time. As we went about unpacking and cleaning, it was the first time in a long time that I had seen her truly happy, but shortly after, she fell ill and called me.

'I feel really ill, Emily. I don't know what's wrong with me. I've got pains in my chest. I might go to A&E.' She had had several panic attacks by then, so it was not unusual, and she had seen a doctor in North Cyprus who told her that every time she had a panic attack, it weakened her heart. We didn't think much of what he said at the time. I drove over to watch the girls, but Faye was back in a couple of hours.

'Why are you back so early?' I asked, surprised; she must have been seen in record time. She dismissed me.

'Oh yeah, nothing's wrong. They discharged me.' I found

out later she had discharged herself without waiting for her blood results. She wanted to get back for the girls.

The next day, I visited her at her new home again and found her in the bath shaving her legs.

'Where are you off to? I thought you were ill?' I said. Faye smiled.

'Oh, I feel a bit better today.' She did look better. There seemed to be an aura around her; she was glowing. We cooked, unpacked some more and made lunch, and then I left to go home for dinner with my family. As I got into the car, Faye waved at me frantically to stop, and I pulled over and slid the window down. She leaned in the car.

'Hold on a minute, will you? I just want to tell you something. Em... life is too short. Just do what you want, Sis, and don't stress about anything, OK?' I laughed and replied,

'Why are you talking like that? You going somewhere?'

'I'm just saying, please live your life and be happy. Life is too short,' she repeated. I was the eldest, the protector, the sensible one; for Faye to give me advice was unheard of.

'Oh, stop being so silly and talking rubbish,' I joked, and drove home still thinking about her odd behaviour. It played on my mind.

At a quarter to 11 that night, I had a call from M, shouting down the phone.

'Something has happened to Faye. Come quick.' I sensed it was bad and drove through the darkened streets at speed, my foot flat to the floor. There were six ambulances, with their blue lights flashing outside Faye's house. I jumped out of the car and pushed my way through the chaos of green-clad paramedics crowded in the little house and went up the stairs. Faye was lying on the floor in her bedroom as a paramedic cut across her throat, trying to get a tube in. Someone was pumping her chest. Her eldest daughter sleepily staggered in from her bedroom and started screaming. I screamed too.

'Somebody please tell me what's going on!' I fell to the floor beside my sister. 'Faye, where do you think you are going? You can't leave me and go. Don't leave us, don't leave us, Faye.' A tear rolled down her cheek. She was gone.

They lifted Faye down the stairs and into the ambulance.

'Why are you taking her to the hospital? Can't you see she's gone?' I was sobbing, screaming hysterically, and then collapsed on the floor. I gathered myself enough to call my daughter and my husband, and we drove to Chase Farm Hospital, where they tried to revive Faye for another 20 minutes. They came out to tell us she had passed away. It did not register. I felt out of my body, unreal, with a thousand insane and mundane thoughts rushing through my head. How was I going to tell everyone? A flood of anger washed over me, and I was inconsolable. I asked for a telephone. I rang Faye's ex-husband at 1.45 a.m. and in a flat voice declared, 'You have won; that bitch and you have got what you wanted. Faye has died because of the pain you put her through. She has died of a broken heart. I will always hold you responsible, you murdering c**t.' I put the phone down.

Mum, Faye and her girls aged 4 and 6

Happy days in Cyprus

Faye, who loved animals

Faye's birthday, September 2008

Emily and Faye, May 2009

5
After Faye

'*Rock bottom became the solid foundation on which I rebuilt my life.*'

J.K. Rowling

It was the early hours of the next morning. The spring light had not yet pushed through the darkness outside the hospital window. The world had taken one more turn, with one less person in it, and I had come to the realisation that I had lost my sister. What was I going to tell my parents, thousands of miles away in North Cyprus? How was I going to tell her beautiful children their mother was no longer with us? It would still be very early there, and I knew every parent dreads a phone call in the middle of the night. I decided I would just tell them Faye was ill, and they had to come straight away.

The phone rang out, and it was our mother that answered. She knew something was wrong immediately, despite what I told her.

'No, Emily, you're lying to me. Faye is not ill. She has died, hasn't she?' I paused, trembling on the edge of that cliff.

'I'm so sorry, Mum.' She started to scream, then hung up the phone. My parents drove straight to the airport, dressed as they were, and got on the next flight. They were with us six hours later, pulling up in front of my house by midday. I am haunted by the memory of my mother getting out of the car, screaming and wailing at the horror of what she was about to face, while the neighbours all came out.

We had to arrange Faye's funeral. It was a mammoth task; family and friends wanted to come from near and far. Everyone was in shock, in disbelief, that she had died so young and tragically at only 35. The house was full every minute of the day with people coming and going. As Faye had died suddenly, there was an autopsy, and we had to wait over 10 days for the results to come back. She had died of a rare heart attack, one in a million for those of her age, and of a type that was hard to detect. We questioned how the hospital could have let her discharge herself with that condition, but they probably wouldn't have discovered it.

The wait for Faye's body was agony. In our culture, a person who has passed must be buried as quickly as possible, and we arranged a ceremony at the mosque. The rituals were usually conducted by volunteer women, but I decided I wanted to wash her body. I was advised not to, but I was determined to do that last ritual for her. My cousin and I went to the mosque's morgue where Faye had been for two weeks. I don't know what I was expecting, but I did not expect to see her looking so beautiful. She had glowing skin and pink cheeks; she looked like an angel, merely sleeping. The body must be wrapped in a certain way with white linen cloths, and you are not usually allowed to kiss them or take anything, but I could not help myself. I cut a lock of her hair to give as a keepsake for her girls, and I kissed my sister goodbye on her forehead and cheeks.

The funeral was exceptional. There were over six hundred people, and they had to block off the roads because the cemetery was full. There was nowhere to stand and barely anywhere to sit. Faye was so adored in the community. Everyone that knew her and knew of her came to that funeral. My sister got the funeral she asked for; we had four white doves in a cage, and when we set them free, they sat on either side of her burial plot, as if they would not leave her.

A tsunami of grief hit me then. I broke down, and for months through that summer I couldn't work, and I could barely function. Faye visited me often in my dreams. I felt her presence so strongly. Her children did not go to their mother's funeral, and afterwards, their father came to pick them up with the woman he left my sister for. After a couple of months, he decided he would take the children to separate them from the grief that had swallowed my family.

In July, he rang to tell me they would stay with his mother in North Cyprus.

'They are my children; they are going to stay with me.' I was shocked.

'But you can't make that decision. Your mother is an old woman. She can't look after them, and they only have their summer clothes with them. It will be winter in North Cyprus soon, and they have school here.' I felt he was just acting out of spite. He had effectively kidnapped them. I immediately contacted the police and the home office, and they launched a case of international abduction. They put his name on a watch list with immigration, so he would be arrested as soon as he stepped back into the UK. I told him we had reported him for abduction, and the police rang him to confirm this and asked him to come back for questioning. It was months before he decided the girls could come back to the UK if I withdrew the complaint about his abduction.

I went to North Cyprus with a letter of intent, showing that I would be responsible for the girls, and brought my nieces back with me. Faye's husband came back to the UK and did have to go to the police for questioning, but as I had withdrawn the complaint, he was released. My mum decided she would go for full custody, so the year after Faye died, we began a court case that lasted three years.

It was a time when I learned much about the children's care system and the legal system. As my mother brought the case and was a pensioner, she was entitled to legal aid. The children's advocacy service had to be involved, with a family lawyer and a social worker. The girls did not have to go to court. Their father did not attend all of the court cases and the court judge complimented my mother; they were so impressed with our drive to gain full custody, and her indomitable spirit after losing her daughter.

'Mrs Sadik – you are a woman to be reckoned with. I suggest the father learn from this and take parental lessons,' they said. Mum won full custody in 2014.

Initially, she and the girls lived with me. She decided she didn't want to return to North Cyprus, as my sister was buried here. Dad moved back too. The stress of the whole affair made my mother very ill. She had heart failure, was literally heartbroken, and transformed into an old woman overnight, with arthritis so bad she couldn't walk. The housing association gave her a ground-floor flat she could live in with the girls. The school had agreed to put the girls back a year of schooling to offer support and give them a chance to catch up. They had lived in North Cyprus for a time, and their English needed developing, so we employed private tutors to give their education a boost.

My daughter was at home studying at college, and her cousins became like her younger sisters. We were there for them with financial and social support, at sports days, parents' evenings and events, and we came together as a family, to bring them up with love. Years went on, and the girls grew up. Considering they had such a difficult childhood, they are now beautiful young women, the eldest studying beauty at college, the youngest working in stables in Hyde Park after studying animal welfare. They still live with us.

Faye's grave, always with fresh flowers

Faye in Cyprus, Summer 2009

6

Founding Serenity Welfare

A new day has come
I was waiting for so long
For a miracle to come
Everyone told me to be strong
Hold on and don't shed a tear
Through the darkness and good times
I knew I'd make it through
And the world thought I had it all
But I was waiting for you
Hush, love
I see a light in the sky
Oh, it's almost blinding me
I can't believe
I've been touched by an angel with love

Let the rain come down and wash away my tears
Let it fill my soul and drown my fears
Let it shatter the walls for a new sun...
A new day has come.'

> *A New Day Has Come*, written by Aldo Nova
> and Stephan Moccio, sung by Celine Dion

By the time I came to terms with the fact Faye had gone, I started to research the care sector. It was so different from the business industry I had known and worked in.

My two nieces were seven and ten when their mother died, and were traumatised. We tried to get support from our local CAMHS (Children's and Adolescent Mental Health Services), but the sessions went so badly we decided not to proceed. The younger one had some understanding and spiritual beliefs that her mother would always be with her. The eldest shut down and did not want to talk about her mum; she internalised it all. At the same time, the legal battle continued for three very emotional years. I met so many people in social services at the time. A friend who worked in the sector took me to one side.

'Emily, I can see you are a good businesswoman. We need a good provision in social care to help securely transport children. For a start, there is a procedure used by some people to transport children in care from one place to another in handcuffs. Did you know that?' I did not, and the news horrified me.

'I don't know enough about this sector. My background is in property,' I said.

'But you do,' she insisted. 'You've just gone through a custody battle. If it wasn't for you, your nieces would have been taken into care; they could have ended up like those children in handcuffs.' I wasn't ready to step into the sector then. I was still grieving; my world was upside down. I told her I couldn't do anything right then, but I would think about it.

It was four years later, in mid-November 2016, that a friend booked us tickets to see the famous American medium John Edward at the Apollo Victoria. He did not come to the UK often, and I was curious to see him live, but I didn't expect anything, especially not a message from Faye. The theatre was packed as we shuffled into our row. The lights went down, and the show started. Suddenly, the whole theatre slowed around me. It was as if someone unspooled a roll of film inside my head, a film about my destiny. As clear as day, I saw the colours of a logo, and the name came to me: Serenity Welfare. It was an epiphany. It felt as if Faye were sending me a message after all and showing me my calling. If Faye hadn't died, there would have been no custodial circumstances, there would have been no Serenity, there would have been no care for those vulnerable children. She is very much a part of our company.

I leant over and whispered to my friend, 'Oh my god, I've got to go home right now.' I knew I needed to get out of there and write it all down. I started registering the logo and the company straight away. I couldn't sit around and wait for someone else to do something; this was a family matter. I committed myself to a whole new way of life.

The care system is challenged in obtaining resources to care for young people, and children often don't have people in their lives who are willing or able to support them. I thought we could do something to change that. I started to learn all I could. I had no idea how the knowledge came so easily to me; it was as if I were an experienced social worker and knew all there was to know. I knew exactly what I needed to do. It's as if I knew children's legislation and I had studied social work. I hadn't studied it; it's instinctive and inherent.

I began with secure transportation, sorting out cars, staff, logo and bank accounts. I invested about £40,000 of my own money into Serenity, as I knew the money would be slow to flow from the local authorities. We needed premises, and when I typed our requirements into Google Offices, a small office in Enfield came up in a business centre. Just before Christmas 2016, I went to have a look. We moved in on Valentine's Day 2017, the day of love, which is at the heart of our ethos.

In the early days, I went out to see how the concept would

be perceived. We started as a secure transportation company for vulnerable children, with handcuffing and restraining very much a last resort, having a nurturing and child-centred approach. I asked the Hertford Mercedes dealership for a credit line to transport children in care in their vehicles. I wanted the prestige and safety of a Mercedes and to offer the children in care a sense of self-worth. As the company was newly established, we had no running accounts, so they called the regional managing director, and I explained our humanistic approach to him. He loved the idea, took a risk and gave us a credit line for one vehicle.

We started with three staff: myself, one support officer and a transport officer. I put an ad on Gumtree to recruit, and they were the ones that responded. I wanted to have staff that were passionate about helping children and young people, but didn't want the uniform and jobsworth, power-happy approach. I wanted our staff to be compassionate and understanding and to have the same skill-set and ethos as myself.

Our first secure transportation was for a looked-after child from a southern England local authority. The child with little bags in chapter one. Our company grew into the care sector after six months when we went up to the Manchester police station to pick up a looked after child from Caerphilly social services in Wales who had absconded to Manchester for weeks. After we collected them, they told me their story. They were a profound self-harmer and had been handcuffed on top of the fresh scars on their wrists in their previous transport. I told them that procedure was totally against what we were about. The transport went well, and we took them to their placement, another care home. A month later I had a phone call from their social worker.

'Remember the young person you brought here in May? Well, they have asked if they can come into your care.' I was shocked at that.

'But we don't have a care home,' I said.

'Well, do you think you can find a home?' They had been up in front of a judge who told them he was putting them under an agreement, which was a deprivation of liberty; they would need to be under 24/7 supervision by two support staff, in a house with window locks and no mobile phone. They were considered a risk to themselves and others, and at risk of being criminally exploited. They asked to go into the care of Serenity Welfare.

'Who are Serenity Welfare, and why would you like to go in their care?' the judge asked. Someone brought him a laptop so he could look at our company website.

'Because Emily and her team are the only company I have come across that understand children in care.' After a few minutes, the court judge replied to this young person.

'I believe this company's values and ethos match the needs of the young person in front of me. Therefore, I am confirming my decision as a temporary placement with Serenity Welfare for the period of three to six months.' As the social worker relayed all this to me, I was stunned, but I knew we couldn't let them down, as it was now a court order.

'What do I have to do?' I asked. The social worker told me to get a package together, as the young person would be attending court in a few weeks' time.

I asked a friend of mine who was going to Germany that summer if we could use her place and rent it off her, as it had to match the requirements of the court order. I got agency staff and friends as support officers to provide the 24-hour care, and I was instructed to go and see the young person the following day in their current setting. When I arrived, they were excited to see me and to be coming into our care.

'Do I have a window in my bedroom?' they asked. It seemed an odd question.

'What do you mean?' I said. They took me to see their room in the children's secure unit in Wales. It was like a cell, with a prison bed, a piece of plastic for a mirror, a hole for a toilet, and no windows. I could see why she was desperate to be somewhere else.

She came to stay, and we embraced her transgender identity and her changed pronouns, stopped her dressing so provocatively and bought her new clothes. She was 15, so we instigated and fought hard to get her education reinstated and get her back to studying for her GCSEs. She moved into semi-independent living when she was 16, our first protégée and success story and a catalyst for us emerging into a different company.

7

Serenity Branches

In a very short space of time, Serenity Welfare developed from a secure transportation provider to a welfare service for children in care, all during our first year of trading. We wanted the company to be a complete welfare service for children, in care and out of it. That provision took shape in our second year, with our location support working for vulnerable children that were under court orders in various settings, like hotels or short-term holiday homes. By then, our workforce had increased, and they provided crisis support 24 hours a day, giving vulnerable children the wrap-around care that is so needed in society these days. In 2018, we launched a mentoring division of bespoke interventions for young people.

My family was always a part of Serenity and Faye's inspiration, and my daughter's practical help was enmeshed in the company. S studied dance and drama at university and was interested in therapy, and she went on to study drama therapy as a master's degree, which she completed in 2022.

I wasn't sure if it was a good idea for her to join us; I knew what it was like to work for your parents, and she needed independent experience first, but by 2018 she has joined as our Head of Mentoring Service, writing interventions and providing therapy tailored to our service users. The working relationship worked!

The company evolved to provide secure transport, mentoring and support work and became part of the National Association of Appropriate Adult Services, trained to support young people in police custody. In 2019, the business was catapulted further as we continued with our passion to nurture and help children and young people with our method of working. We were recognised in the industry, and had repeat business from local authorities and requests from our service's users, our young people. We had outgrown our little offices in Enfield, where we had eight office staff crammed into a small space. I decided we needed to move. I had a vision of us operating from a multi-function base, somewhere that could be called Serenity Village. A community where young people could use our services and live on site, and use the grounds and recreational facilities. I never thought I would find somewhere like it so quickly.

I was sitting in my garden on a mild December day in 2019, flicking through my phone browsing commercial properties, when a photograph of a beautiful manor house popped up. I couldn't believe it was a commercial building, but I thought I would chance it and rang the agent. I explained who Serenity Welfare were and what we were looking for. They promised to speak to the landlord. I drove over to Broxbourne and met the landlord at the house, who embraced what we had achieved and what we wanted to do. We agreed on terms, and by 13th February 2020, we had moved, lock, stock and barrel, to our new home.

It is a large house, with sweeping front lawns, where you can spot occasional deer wandering across under pink clouds at the end of the day. The drawing room is spacious, but comfortable, with the grand fireplace, Chinese vases and plush sofas of a country house, yet it is warm and welcoming and feels like a home. It is not an imposing house; it has a good feel to it, with gardens and grounds that can accommodate our transport services, a separate cottage for young people to have a respite break, a spacious kitchen, a sweeping staircase, a games room with a full-size snooker table and a gravel drive. Built in 1745 by the parish, with a link to the Foundling Museum in London, it had a philanthropic purpose and was once a children's home. It is a peaceful place, a place of serenity, perfect for our office and for the most vulnerable children to escape to.

We moved in just before a national lockdown amidst a worldwide Coronavirus pandemic. Yet because we were self-contained and exercising social distancing, we could continue working at the one site. We created separate areas, had the vehicles and the office sanitised and worked in conjunction with social distancing in masks. The building saved our company; it meant we could get on with our unique work, while other businesses had to close.

Serenity continued to grow at this difficult time. In 2020 I engaged a PR firm to help promote the Hope Instead of Handcuffs Campaign, and we had a coalition of MPs and peers on board. I wanted to stop the transportation of children and young people in the care system who are deemed 'high-risk' (perhaps with a history of self-harm, ADHD or being gang-affiliated) in handcuffs or caged vehicles similar to a police van. Those children and young people had already faced so much trauma in their lives; I did not believe they should be treated in a way that is dehumanising.

Back in 2017, our practice was unheard of. I'm delighted to say we have come a long way. We have 36 MPs backing the campaign, demanding the government ban the practice routinely used by some operators, 'unless there is a considerable risk of the child harming themselves or others'. Its signatories include MP Steve McCabe, chair of the APPG on looked after children and care leavers, six House of Lord members and other influential people. I have been pressuring for the campaign to continue throughout the pandemic, speaking to senior civil servants in the Department of Education, the national director of Ofsted social care, the children's commissioner's office and senior MPs, to ascertain who is responsible for passing the bill in parliament. The campaign also calls for a ministerial post to support the mentoring of vulnerable children and implement early intervention.

Serenity Welfare commissioned a report, Lives Transformed, Potential Fulfilled (which is on our website), by a government analyst to demonstrate to the UK government how they would save money by employing long-term thinking and dealing with smaller issues, and how this can have a social impact across our wider society. They took notice of the report but have not yet actioned it. The campaign for Hope Instead of Handcuffs grew in momentum too. It may have slowed due to the pandemic, but it has not stopped. We will get there.

We continue to develop. In 2022, we launched our legal division Serenity Legal Services, registered with statutory law bodies (the SRA) to represent children and young people in criminal law and provide an advocacy service, together with civil law, family law and refugee and asylum-seeking services.

Our next challenge for 2022 is to launch a charity, Faye's Way, in the name of my sister, which we have registered with the charity commission. Faye had a lot to do with why Serenity Welfare was founded, and the charity will be her legacy, in remembrance of her and her love for children. Faye's Way will be run by a youth panel and overseen by senior management. There will be an apprenticeship scheme formulated with companies we already work with, and we even have our own scheme for inspiring future-generation transport officers and mentors. The charity will give life skills to young people referred by the local authority and other organisations, building their confidence and self-worth.

The charity will be located in a building in North London that has a good structure with showers and decent facilities, where we will provide hygiene opportunities and career coaching. I plan to open a charity shop on the high street, which will incorporate a coffee shop run by young people. It will be a cash-free environment. Customers will use a Faye's Way card that can be topped up at our facility, exclusive to Faye's Way to be used only in our shop.

I have a three-year vision for the whole charity, based on central values and the three top tips for career development that I practiced in my previous career.

1. Change is good. Just because something has been done a certain way for decades doesn't mean it's right. If you think something can be done better, then make it happen.
2. Take some time to decide on your values. They will help guide your work and can be referred to if you're unsure.
3. Be brave and never give up. There be many things that you doubt, but trust your ability. Anything is possible if you believe in what you are doing and do it with passion.

Recently, I returned from a short holiday in North Cyprus with my elderly parents. As I stepped off the plane, I discovered that I was the finalist for Best Business Woman of the year in the children and families category, 2021. I knew I had been shortlisted, but I never expected to win. I was invited to the gala event in the Hilton at Wembley with some of the team from Serenity, and it was a lovely evening, like a BAFTA awards ceremony, with the red carpet and stage, and we all scrubbed up well! I was called up to collect my glittering glass and gold trophy and felt very humbled that we had been recognized for making a positive impact on the lives of young people. In 2020 we were also given the best practice award in the health and social care parliamentary review.

Throughout the development of Serenity Welfare, I've held to the core values we started with. I believe in nurturing my staff; without them I wouldn't have a company. You need good people around you. They call me boss lady! If I am the boss, I hold to my philosophy that leaders must understand the everyday trials and tribulations of their staff working on the front lines in order to be able to lead effectively by doing the job yourself first, which I did in the early days of Serenity.

Our wonderful company goes from strength to strength, word has spread, and I've had people from America contacting me and asking if we could assist them there in their district counties. We've had recognition from government officials, the public sector and the media. But we would not be here without the loss of my lovely sister, or without the love and support of family, and that ethos is what we must stand by; an open, honest, reliable, anti-oppressive, anti-discriminatory practice, which I have held to throughout my life story. **To treat each other with kindness and humanity, to treat people how you would want to be treated, irrespective of race, colour or religion**. This is the Serenity Welfare Mission Statement.

You can find out more about Serenity Welfare and our work by reading the news articles linked from our website:

https://serenitywelfare.org/

All proceeds from the sales of The Road to Serenity will be donated to the Faye's Way charity

Emily Aklan, April 2017

Serenity Welfare brochure

Our Serenity Welfare logo

Our fantastic CEO, Emily, presenting Serenity Welfare's services to local authorities.

Emily presenting to local authorities at the Westminster forum, 2018

Winning the Best Business Women Award for 2021 for Families and Children Category

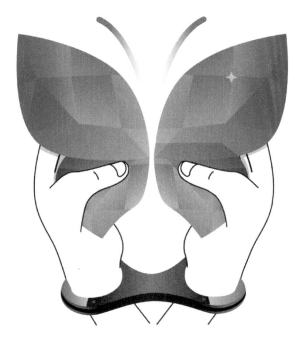

Hope Instead of Handcuffs

Hope instead of Handcuffs logo, designed by a young person in care

Faye's Way logo

Emily Aklan, CEO & FOUNDER of Serenity Welfare

"Whilst we nurture our clients, it is equally important you nurture and look after your staff. Because without them you don't have a business."

Emily Aklan
CEO - Serenity Welfare

Emily golden nugget quote

Printed in Great Britain
by Amazon

86005871R00054